Flavors of Goa
A Culinary Journey Through the Most Popular Dishes

Introduction

Welcome to "Flavors of Goa: A Culinary Journey Through the Most Popular Dishes," an eBook that invites you to explore the vibrant and diverse culinary landscape of one of India's most enchanting regions. Nestled along the picturesque coastline of the Arabian Sea, Goa is renowned for its sun-kissed beaches, lush landscapes, and, of course, its rich and flavorful cuisine.

In this eBook, we embark on a gastronomic adventure through the heart of Goa, unveiling a collection of the region's most beloved and iconic dishes. From succulent seafood curries to aromatic spice-infused rice, Goa's cuisine is a celebration of bold flavors, unique ingredients, and a melting pot of cultural influences.

Join us as we delve into the recipes that have been passed down through generations, each dish telling a story of the cultural tapestry that defines Goan cuisine. Whether you are an aspiring home cook eager to recreate the magic of Goan kitchens or a food enthusiast looking to savor the essence of this coastal paradise, this eBook is your guide to mastering the art of Goan cooking.

Prepare your senses for an exploration of tantalizing spices, fresh seafood, tropical fruits, and the warm hospitality that defines the spirit of Goa. Get ready to bring the taste of Goa into your own kitchen and experience the joy of creating these delectable dishes that have stood the test of time.

Come, let's embark on a culinary journey through the alleys of Goa, where each recipe is a celebration of tradition, flavor, and the irresistible charm that makes Goan cuisine truly exceptional.

Index

1.Fish Curry Rice

Goan Fish Curry Rice Recipe

Ingredients

For Fish Curry:

- 500g fish (preferably a firm-fleshed variety like kingfish or mackerel)
- 1 cup grated coconut
- 1 large onion, finely chopped
- 2 medium-sized tomatoes, chopped
- 1 small piece of tamarind (soaked in water)
- 2-3 green chilies, slit
- 1 sprig curry leaves
- 1 teaspoon mustard seeds
- 1 teaspoon cumin seeds
- 1 teaspoon turmeric powder
- 1 tablespoon red chili powder
- 1 tablespoon coriander powder
- Salt to taste
- 2 tablespoons oil

For Rice:

- 1 cup basmati rice
- 2 cups water
- Salt to taste

Instructions

Step 1: Prepare the Fish

- Clean and wash the fish thoroughly. If using whole fish, ensure they are scaled and gutted. Cut into medium-sized pieces.
- Marinate the fish with half a teaspoon of turmeric powder and salt. Allow it to marinate for at least 15-20 minutes.

Step 2: Make the Spice Paste

- In a blender, combine grated coconut, chopped onion, mustard seeds, cumin seeds, red chili powder, coriander powder, and the soaked tamarind. Blend to a smooth paste, adding water as needed.

Step 3: Prepare the Base for Curry

- Heat oil in a pan. Add curry leaves and slit green chilies. Sauté for a minute.
- Add chopped tomatoes and cook until they turn soft and the oil begins to separate.
- Now, add the spice paste from the blender. Cook on medium heat, stirring continuously, until the raw smell disappears and the masala releases oil.

Step 4: Add Fish to the Curry

- Pour water to achieve the desired curry consistency. Bring the curry to a gentle boil.
- Add the marinated fish pieces, ensuring they are well-coated with the curry. Be gentle to avoid breaking the fish pieces.
- Simmer on low heat until the fish is cooked through. This usually takes about 10-15 minutes. Adjust the salt as needed.

Step 5: Cook the Rice

- While the fish curry is simmering, wash and soak the basmati rice for 20 minutes.
- In a separate pot, bring water to a boil. Add salt and soaked rice. Cook until the rice is fluffy and each grain is separate.

Step 6: Serve

- Once the fish is cooked, garnish the curry with fresh coriander leaves.
- Serve the Goan Fish Curry hot over a bed of steamed basmati rice.

Tips:
- Adjust the spice levels according to your preference by controlling the amount of red chili powder and green chilies.

- Use fresh fish for the best flavor, and you can experiment with different types of fish based on your availability and preference.
- For an extra layer of flavor, you can add a tempering of mustard seeds and curry leaves in hot oil and pour it over the curry before serving.

Enjoy this traditional Goan Fish Curry Rice, a flavorful and comforting dish that perfectly balances the richness of coconut, the tanginess of tamarind, and the natural goodness of fresh fish.

2.Prawn Balchão

Goan Prawn Balchão Recipe

Ingredients

- 500g prawns, cleaned and deveined
- 10-12 dry red chilies (Kashmiri chilies for color, and spicy chilies for heat)
- 1 cup chopped onions
- 1/2 cup chopped tomatoes
- 1/4 cup tamarind pulp
- 1/4 cup vinegar
- 1 tablespoon sugar
- 1 teaspoon turmeric powder
- 1 teaspoon mustard seeds
- 1 teaspoon cumin seeds
- 1 teaspoon fenugreek seeds
- 1 tablespoon peppercorns
- 8-10 garlic cloves
- 1-inch ginger, finely chopped
- 4-5 cloves

- 4-5 green cardamom pods
- 1 cinnamon stick
- Salt to taste
- 3-4 tablespoons oil

Instructions

Step 1: Prepare the Prawns

- Clean and devein the prawns, leaving the tails intact for presentation.
- Marinate the prawns with half a teaspoon of turmeric powder and a pinch of salt. Allow them to marinate for at least 15-20 minutes.

Step 2: Prepare the Spice Paste

- Soak the dry red chilies in warm water for about 15-20 minutes to soften them.
- In a blender, combine soaked red chilies, garlic cloves, ginger, mustard seeds, cumin seeds, fenugreek seeds, peppercorns, and a little water. Blend into a smooth paste.

Step 3: Cook the Balchão Base

- Heat oil in a pan. Add cloves, green cardamom pods, and cinnamon stick. Sauté for a minute until they release their aroma.
- Add chopped onions and cook until they become golden brown.
- Add the spice paste from the blender and cook on medium heat, stirring continuously, until the raw smell disappears, and the masala releases oil.

Step 4: Add Tomatoes and Prawns

- Add chopped tomatoes to the pan and cook until they become soft and the oil begins to separate.

- Now, add the marinated prawns to the masala. Cook for 3-4 minutes until the prawns turn opaque.

Step 5: Add Tamarind, Vinegar, and Sugar

- Mix tamarind pulp, vinegar, and sugar in a bowl. Add this mixture to the prawns, stirring well.
- Adjust the salt according to your taste. Balchão is known for its balance of spicy, tangy, and slightly sweet flavors.

Step 6: Simmer and Cook

- Reduce the heat to low and let the prawns simmer in the flavorful masala for another 10-15 minutes, allowing them to absorb the spices.

Step 7: Final Touch

- Once the prawns are cooked through and the masala has thickened, check the seasoning and adjust if needed.
- Garnish with fresh coriander leaves and remove from heat.

Step 8: Serve

- Allow the Prawn Balchão to rest for a few minutes before serving. It pairs well with steamed rice or crusty bread.

Tips:

- You can adjust the spice level by controlling the quantity of red chilies. For a milder version, use fewer spicy chilies.
- The balance of sweetness from sugar, tanginess from tamarind, and acidity from vinegar is crucial to the flavor profile of Prawn Balchão.

Enjoy this authentic Goan Prawn Balchão, a spicy and tangy delicacy that perfectly showcases the bold flavors of Goan cuisine.

3.Chicken Cafreal

Goan Chicken Cafreal Recipe

Ingredients

For Chicken Marinade:

- 1 kg chicken pieces (preferably with bones for more flavor)
- 2 tablespoons ginger-garlic paste
- 1 tablespoon lime juice
- Salt to taste

For Green Masala:

- 2 cups fresh coriander leaves, chopped
- 1 cup fresh mint leaves, chopped
- 8-10 green chilies (adjust according to spice preference)
- 6-8 garlic cloves
- 1-inch ginger, chopped
- 1 teaspoon cumin seeds
- 1 teaspoon black peppercorns

- 1 teaspoon turmeric powder
- 1 tablespoon coriander powder
- 1 tablespoon lime juice
- Salt to taste
- Water (as needed for grinding)

Other Ingredients:

- 2-3 tablespoons oil
- 1 tablespoon vinegar
- Salt to taste

Instructions

Step 1: Marinate the Chicken

- Clean and wash the chicken pieces. Pat them dry with a paper towel.
- In a large bowl, mix ginger-garlic paste, lime juice, and salt. Coat the chicken pieces with this marinade and let it rest for at least 30 minutes.

Step 2: Prepare the Green Masala

- In a blender, combine fresh coriander leaves, mint leaves, green chilies, garlic cloves, ginger, cumin seeds, black peppercorns, turmeric powder, coriander powder, lime juice, and salt.

- Add a little water and blend into a smooth paste. Adjust the consistency by adding more water if needed.

Step 3: Marinate the Chicken with Green Masala

- Coat the marinated chicken pieces with the freshly prepared green masala. Ensure each piece is well-covered with the flavorful masala.
- Allow the chicken to marinate for at least 2-3 hours, or preferably overnight in the refrigerator, for the flavors to penetrate.

Step 4: Grill the Chicken

- Preheat your grill or oven to a medium-high temperature.
- Place the marinated chicken pieces on the grill or in the oven, allowing them to cook until they are charred and cooked through. Turn the pieces occasionally for even cooking.
- If using an oven, you can also broil the chicken for a few minutes at the end for that extra charred effect.

Step 5: Prepare the Cafreal Sauce

- In a pan, heat oil. Add any remaining green masala from the marination process and cook it for a few minutes until the raw smell disappears.
- Add vinegar and salt to taste. Cook for another 2-3 minutes, creating a flavorful sauce.

Step 6: Coat Grilled Chicken with Cafreal Sauce

- Once the chicken pieces are grilled to perfection, transfer them to the pan with the Cafreal sauce.
- Coat each chicken piece with the sauce, allowing it to absorb the rich flavors.

Step 7: Serve

- Garnish with fresh coriander leaves and lime wedges.
- Serve the Chicken Cafreal hot, either as a standalone dish or with a side of bread or rice.

Tips:

- Chicken Cafreal is traditionally a spicy dish, but you can adjust the level of green chilies according to your taste preferences.
- Marinating the chicken overnight enhances the flavors, but if you're short on time, a few hours will still yield delicious results.

Enjoy this aromatic and flavorful Goan Chicken Cafreal, a delightful dish that showcases the vibrant essence of coriander, mint, and Goan spices.

4.Sorak Curry

Goan Sorak Curry Recipe

Ingredients

For Sorak Curry Base:

- 1 cup freshly grated coconut
- 1 large onion, finely chopped
- 2 medium-sized tomatoes, chopped
- 2-3 green chilies, chopped
- 1-inch ginger, chopped
- 6-8 garlic cloves
- 1 tablespoon tamarind pulp
- 1 teaspoon mustard seeds
- 1 teaspoon cumin seeds
- 1/2 teaspoon fenugreek seeds
- 1 teaspoon turmeric powder
- 1 tablespoon red chili powder
- 1 tablespoon coriander powder
- Salt to taste
- 2 tablespoons oil

For the Curry:

- 500g fish or shrimp (cleaned and deveined)
- 1 cup water (adjust as needed)

- Fresh coriander leaves for garnish

Instructions
Step 1: Prepare Sorak Curry Base

- In a pan, heat 1 tablespoon of oil over medium heat. Add mustard seeds, cumin seeds, and fenugreek seeds. Allow them to splutter.
- Add chopped onions and sauté until they turn golden brown.
- Add chopped green chilies, ginger, and garlic. Sauté for a couple of minutes until the raw smell disappears.
- Add freshly grated coconut to the pan and roast until it turns golden brown. Stir continuously to avoid burning.
- Once the coconut is roasted, add chopped tomatoes and cook until they become soft and the oil starts to separate.
- Add tamarind pulp, turmeric powder, red chili powder, coriander powder, and salt. Mix well and cook for another 2-3 minutes.

Step 2: Blend into a Smooth Paste

- Allow the mixture to cool slightly. Transfer it to a blender and blend into a smooth paste. Add water if needed to achieve a smooth consistency.

Step 3: Prepare the Curry

- In the same pan, heat the remaining 1 tablespoon of oil. Pour the blended sorak curry base into the pan.
- Add 1 cup of water to the pan, adjusting the consistency of the curry according to your preference. Bring it to a gentle boil.

Step 4: Add Fish or Shrimp

- Once the curry base is simmering, add the cleaned fish or shrimp to the pan.
- Allow the fish or shrimp to cook in the curry, absorbing the flavors. This usually takes about 10-15 minutes, depending on the size and type of seafood.

Step 5: Adjust Seasoning

- Taste the curry and adjust the salt and spice levels according to your preference. You can also add more tamarind pulp for extra tanginess.

Step 6: Garnish and Serve

- Once the fish or shrimp are cooked through, garnish the Sorak Curry with fresh coriander leaves.
- Remove from heat and let it rest for a few minutes before serving.

Tips:

- Sorak Curry is traditionally served with rice. It pairs well with both white rice and Goan red rice.
- You can use a mix of different fish or shrimp for added variety and flavor.
- Experiment with the level of spiciness by adjusting the quantity of green chilies and red chili powder.

Enjoy this tangy and spicy Goan Sorak Curry, a delightful dish that brings together the richness of coconut, the tanginess of tamarind, and the goodness of seafood.

5.Goan Fish Curry

Goan Fish Curry Recipe

Ingredients

For Fish Marinade:

- 500g fish pieces (preferably a firm-fleshed variety like kingfish or mackerel)
- 1 teaspoon turmeric powder
- Salt to taste

For Curry Base:

- 1 cup freshly grated coconut
- 1 large onion, finely chopped
- 2 medium-sized tomatoes, chopped
- 2-3 green chilies, chopped
- 1-inch ginger, chopped
- 6-8 garlic cloves
- 1 tablespoon tamarind pulp
- 1 teaspoon mustard seeds
- 1 teaspoon cumin seeds
- 1/2 teaspoon fenugreek seeds
- 1 teaspoon turmeric powder
- 1 tablespoon red chili powder
- 1 tablespoon coriander powder
- Salt to taste
- 2 tablespoons oil

For Tempering:

- 1 tablespoon oil
- 1 teaspoon mustard seeds
- 2-3 dried red chilies
- Few curry leaves

Additional Ingredients:

- Tamarind pulp (if needed for extra tanginess)
- Fresh coriander leaves for garnish

Instructions

Step 1: Marinate the Fish

- Clean and wash the fish pieces. Pat them dry with a paper towel.
- Marinate the fish with turmeric powder and salt. Allow it to marinate for at least 15-20 minutes.

Step 2: Prepare Curry Base

- In a pan, heat 2 tablespoons of oil over medium heat. Add mustard seeds, cumin seeds, and fenugreek seeds. Allow them to splutter.
- Add chopped onions and sauté until they turn golden brown.
- Add chopped green chilies, ginger, and garlic. Sauté for a couple of minutes until the raw smell disappears.
- Add freshly grated coconut to the pan and roast until it turns golden brown. Stir continuously to avoid burning.
- Once the coconut is roasted, add chopped tomatoes and cook until they become soft and the oil starts to separate.
- Add tamarind pulp, turmeric powder, red chili powder, coriander powder, and salt. Mix well and cook for another 2-3 minutes.

Step 3: Blend into a Smooth Paste

- Allow the mixture to cool slightly. Transfer it to a blender and blend into a smooth paste. Add water if needed to achieve a smooth consistency.

Step 4: Prepare the Curry

- In the same pan, heat oil for tempering. Add mustard seeds, dried red chilies, and curry leaves. Let them splutter and release their flavors.
- Pour the blended curry base into the pan. Add water to achieve the desired curry consistency. Bring it to a gentle boil.

Step 5: Add the Marinated Fish

- Once the curry base is simmering, gently add the marinated fish pieces to the pan.
- Allow the fish to cook in the curry, absorbing the rich flavors. This usually takes about 10-15 minutes, depending on the size and type of fish.

Step 6: Adjust Seasoning

- Taste the curry and adjust the salt and spice levels according to your preference. If you prefer a tangier curry, you can add more tamarind pulp.

Step 7: Garnish and Serve

- Once the fish is cooked through and the curry has thickened, garnish the Goan Fish Curry with fresh coriander leaves.
- Remove from heat and let it rest for a few minutes before serving.

Tips:

- Goan Fish Curry is traditionally served with rice. It pairs well with both white rice and Goan red rice.
- Experiment with the choice of fish. Firm-fleshed fish works best for this curry.
- Adjust the spice levels by varying the quantity of green chilies and red chili powder.

Enjoy this authentic Goan Fish Curry, a delicious blend of coconut, tamarind, and aromatic spices that captures the essence of Goan cuisine.

6.Prawn Curry Rice

Goan Prawn Curry Rice Recipe

Ingredients

For Prawn Marinade:

- 500g prawns, cleaned and deveined
- 1 teaspoon turmeric powder

- Salt to taste

For Curry Base:

- 1 cup freshly grated coconut
- 1 large onion, finely chopped
- 2 medium-sized tomatoes, chopped
- 2-3 green chilies, chopped
- 1-inch ginger, chopped
- 6-8 garlic cloves
- 1 tablespoon tamarind pulp
- 1 teaspoon mustard seeds
- 1 teaspoon cumin seeds
- 1/2 teaspoon fenugreek seeds
- 1 teaspoon turmeric powder
- 1 tablespoon red chili powder
- 1 tablespoon coriander powder
- Salt to taste
- 2 tablespoons oil

For Tempering:

- 1 tablespoon oil
- 1 teaspoon mustard seeds
- 2-3 dried red chilies

- Few curry leaves

Additional Ingredients:

- Tamarind pulp (if needed for extra tanginess)
- Fresh coriander leaves for garnish

Instructions
Step 1: Marinate the Prawns

- Clean and devein the prawns, leaving the tails intact for presentation.
- Marinate the prawns with turmeric powder and salt. Allow them to marinate for at least 15-20 minutes.

Step 2: Prepare Curry Base

- In a pan, heat 2 tablespoons of oil over medium heat. Add mustard seeds, cumin seeds, and fenugreek seeds. Allow them to splutter.
- Add chopped onions and sauté until they turn golden brown.
- Add chopped green chilies, ginger, and garlic. Sauté for a couple of minutes until the raw smell disappears.
- Add freshly grated coconut to the pan and roast until it turns golden brown. Stir continuously to avoid burning.
- Once the coconut is roasted, add chopped tomatoes and cook until they become soft and the oil starts to separate.

- Add tamarind pulp, turmeric powder, red chili powder, coriander powder, and salt. Mix well and cook for another 2-3 minutes.

Step 3: Blend into a Smooth Paste

- Allow the mixture to cool slightly. Transfer it to a blender and blend into a smooth paste. Add water if needed to achieve a smooth consistency.

Step 4: Prepare the Curry

- In the same pan, heat oil for tempering. Add mustard seeds, dried red chilies, and curry leaves. Let them splutter and release their flavors.
- Pour the blended curry base into the pan. Add water to achieve the desired curry consistency. Bring it to a gentle boil.

Step 5: Add the Marinated Prawns

- Once the curry base is simmering, gently add the marinated prawns to the pan.
- Allow the prawns to cook in the curry, absorbing the rich flavors. This usually takes about 5-7 minutes, depending on the size of the prawns.

Step 6: Adjust Seasoning

- Taste the curry and adjust the salt and spice levels according to your preference. If you prefer a tangier curry, you can add more tamarind pulp.

Step 7: Garnish and Serve

- Once the prawns are cooked through and the curry has thickened, garnish the Goan Prawn Curry with fresh coriander leaves.
- Remove from heat and let it rest for a few minutes before serving.

Tips:
- Goan Prawn Curry is traditionally served with rice. It pairs well with both white rice and Goan red rice.
- Adjust the spice levels by varying the quantity of green chilies and red chili powder.
- To enhance the flavor, you can also add a splash of coconut milk towards the end of cooking.

Enjoy this delicious Goan Prawn Curry Rice, a delightful dish that captures the flavors of coconut, tamarind, and succulent prawns in a rich and aromatic curry.

7.Xacuti (Chicken or Vegetarian)

Goan Xacuti Recipe

Ingredients

For Chicken or Vegetable Marinade:

- 500g chicken pieces (bone-in for more flavor) or mixed vegetables (cauliflower, carrots, peas, potatoes)
- 1 teaspoon turmeric powder
- Salt to taste

For Xacuti Spice Paste:

- 1 cup freshly grated coconut
- 1 large onion, finely chopped
- 2 medium-sized tomatoes, chopped
- 2-3 green chilies
- 1-inch ginger, chopped
- 6-8 garlic cloves
- 1 tablespoon tamarind pulp
- 1 tablespoon oil

For Roasted Spice Powder:

- 1 tablespoon coriander seeds
- 1 teaspoon cumin seeds
- 1/2 teaspoon fennel seeds

- 1/2 teaspoon poppy seeds
- 1-inch cinnamon stick
- 4-5 cloves
- 4-5 black peppercorns
- 4-5 dried red chilies (adjust according to spice preference)

For Curry:

- 2 tablespoons oil
- 1 large onion, finely sliced
- 1 teaspoon mustard seeds
- 1 sprig curry leaves
- Salt to taste
- Fresh coriander leaves for garnish

Instructions
Step 1: Marinate the Chicken or Vegetables

- Clean and wash the chicken pieces or vegetables. If using chicken, leave the bones for added flavor.
- Marinate the chicken or vegetables with turmeric powder and salt. Allow them to marinate for at least 15-20 minutes.

Step 2: Roast the Spices

- In a dry pan, roast coriander seeds, cumin seeds, fennel seeds, poppy seeds, cinnamon stick, cloves, black peppercorns, and dried red chilies over medium heat.
- Roast until the spices release their aroma and turn slightly brown. Be careful not to burn them.
- Allow the roasted spices to cool and then grind them into a fine powder using a spice grinder or mortar and pestle.

Step 3: Prepare the Xacuti Spice Paste

- In the same pan, heat 1 tablespoon of oil. Add chopped onions, green chilies, ginger, and garlic. Sauté until the onions are golden brown.
- Add freshly grated coconut to the pan and roast until it turns golden brown. Stir continuously to avoid burning.
- Add chopped tomatoes and cook until they become soft and the oil starts to separate.
- Add the roasted spice powder to the pan and mix well. Cook for another 2-3 minutes.

Step 4: Blend into a Smooth Paste

- Allow the mixture to cool slightly. Transfer it to a blender and add tamarind pulp. Blend into a smooth paste. Add water if needed to achieve a smooth consistency.

Step 5: Cook the Chicken or Vegetables

- In a large pan or pot, heat 2 tablespoons of oil. Add mustard seeds and curry leaves. Let them splutter.
- Add sliced onions and sauté until they turn golden brown.
- If using chicken, add the marinated chicken pieces and cook until they are browned on all sides.
- If using vegetables, add the mixed vegetables and sauté for a few minutes.

Step 6: Add Xacuti Spice Paste

- Pour the Xacuti spice paste into the pan with chicken or vegetables. Mix well, ensuring that every piece is coated with the flavorful masala.

Step 7: Cook the Curry

- Add water to achieve the desired curry consistency. Bring it to a gentle boil, then reduce the heat to low and let it simmer until the chicken or vegetables are cooked through. This usually takes about 15-20 minutes.

Step 8: Adjust Seasoning

- Taste the curry and adjust the salt according to your preference. If you like it tangier, you can add more tamarind pulp.

Step 9: Garnish and Serve

- Once the chicken or vegetables are cooked and the curry has thickened, garnish the Goan Xacuti with fresh coriander leaves.
- Remove from heat and let it rest for a few minutes before serving.

Tips:

- Goan Xacuti is traditionally served with rice or bread. It pairs well with both white rice and Goan red rice.
- You can adjust the spice levels by varying the quantity of dried red chilies in the spice paste.

Enjoy this flavorful Goan Xacuti, a delicious curry that brings together the richness of roasted spices, coconut, and either succulent chicken or mixed vegetables.

8.Sannas

Goan Sannas Recipe

Ingredients

For Sannas Batter:

- 2 cups raw rice

- 1 cup cooked rice
- 1 cup grated coconut
- 1/4 cup sugar
- 1/2 teaspoon salt
- 1 teaspoon yeast
- 1/4 cup warm water

For Steaming:

- Sannas moulds or idli moulds
- Water for steaming

Instructions
Step 1: Soak the Rice

- Wash the raw rice thoroughly and soak it in water for at least 4-6 hours or overnight.
- Drain the soaked rice and keep it aside.

Step 2: Prepare Yeast Mixture

- In a small bowl, dissolve 1 teaspoon of yeast in 1/4 cup of warm water. Allow it to sit for 5-10 minutes until it becomes frothy.

Step 3: Grind the Batter

- In a blender, combine the soaked raw rice, cooked rice, grated coconut, sugar, and salt.
- Add the yeast mixture to the blender and blend everything into a smooth batter. Add a little water if needed to achieve a thick but pourable consistency.

Step 4: Ferment the Batter

Pour the batter into a large bowl and cover it with a clean cloth. Allow the batter to ferment in a warm place for 6-8 hours or overnight. The batter should rise and become slightly airy.

Step 5: Prepare Sannas Moulds

- Grease the sannas moulds or idli moulds with a little oil to prevent sticking.

Step 6: Steam the Sannas

- Fill each mould with the fermented batter until it's about 3/4 full. This allows room for the sannas to rise during steaming.
- Heat water in the steamer or idli steamer until it begins to boil.
- Place the filled moulds in the steamer, cover, and steam for about 15-20 minutes or until a toothpick inserted into the center comes out clean.

Step 7: Serve the Sannas

- Once the sannas are cooked, remove them from the moulds and let them cool for a few minutes.
- Serve the fluffy sannas hot, accompanied by your favorite chicken curry or any other curry of your choice.

Tips:

- Sannas pairs exceptionally well with Goan Chicken Curry or any other spicy curry.
- The consistency of the batter is crucial for the sannas to rise properly during steaming. It should be thick but pourable.
- You can adjust the sweetness of the sannas by varying the amount of sugar according to your taste preference.

Enjoy these light and fluffy Goan Sannas, a perfect accompaniment to complement the rich and flavorful taste of Goan chicken curry or any curry you choose

9.Rava Fried Fish

Goan Rava Fried Fish Recipe

Ingredients

For Marinating the Fish:

- 500g fish fillets (use a firm-fleshed variety like kingfish or pomfret)
- 1 teaspoon turmeric powder
- 1 teaspoon red chili powder
- 1 teaspoon ginger-garlic paste
- Salt to taste
- 1 tablespoon lime juice

For Coating:

- 1 cup semolina (rava/sooji)
- 1/2 cup rice flour
- Salt to taste
- 1/2 teaspoon turmeric powder
- 1/2 teaspoon red chili powder

For Frying:

- Vegetable oil for shallow frying

For Garnish:

- Fresh coriander leaves (optional)
- Lemon wedges

Instructions

Step 1: Marinate the Fish

- Clean and wash the fish fillets. Pat them dry with a paper towel.
- In a bowl, combine turmeric powder, red chili powder, ginger-garlic paste, salt, and lime juice to create a smooth marinade.
- Coat each fish fillet with the marinade, ensuring they are well-covered. Allow the fish to marinate for at least 30 minutes, allowing the flavors to infuse.

Step 2: Prepare the Coating Mixture

- In a shallow dish, combine semolina, rice flour, salt, turmeric powder, and red chili powder. Mix the dry ingredients thoroughly to create the coating mixture.

Step 3: Coat the Fish

- Heat oil in a frying pan over medium heat. Ensure the oil is hot before adding the fish.
- Take each marinated fish fillet and coat it generously with the semolina mixture. Press the coating onto the fish to make it adhere well.

Step 4: Fry the Fish

- Carefully place the coated fish fillets into the hot oil, ensuring not to overcrowd the pan. Fry each side until it turns golden brown and crispy. This usually takes about 3-4 minutes per side, depending on the thickness of the fillets.
- Use a slotted spoon to remove the fried fish from the oil and place them on a plate lined with paper towels to absorb any excess oil.

Step 5: Garnish and Serve

- Garnish the Rava Fried Fish with fresh coriander leaves (optional) and serve hot.
- Serve with lemon wedges on the side for a burst of freshness.

Tips:
- Ensure that the oil is hot before adding the fish to achieve a crispy coating.
- You can adjust the level of spiciness by varying the amount of red chili powder in the marinade and coating mixture.
- Use a firm-fleshed fish variety for better results, as it holds up well during the frying process.

Enjoy this delightful Goan Rava Fried Fish as a perfect seafood snack or appetizer, showcasing the crispiness of the semolina coating and the flavorful spices that make it a favorite among seafood enthusiasts.

10.Crispy Goan Prawns

Crispy Goan Prawns Recipe

Ingredients

For Prawn Marinade:

- 500g large prawns, cleaned and deveined
- 1 teaspoon turmeric powder
- 1 teaspoon red chili powder
- 1 teaspoon ginger-garlic paste
- Salt to taste
- 1 tablespoon lime juice

For Coating:

- 1 cup semolina (rava/sooji)
- 1/2 cup rice flour
- 1/2 cup all-purpose flour (maida)
- Salt to taste
- 1/2 teaspoon turmeric powder
- 1/2 teaspoon red chili powder

For Frying:

- Vegetable oil for deep frying

For Garnish:

- Fresh coriander leaves (optional)
- Lemon wedges

Instructions
Step 1: Prepare the Prawn Marinade

- Clean and devein the prawns, leaving the tails intact for presentation.
- In a bowl, mix turmeric powder, red chili powder, ginger-garlic paste, salt, and lime juice to create a smooth marinade.
- Coat each prawn with the marinade, ensuring they are well-covered. Allow the prawns to marinate for at least 30 minutes to let the flavors infuse.

Step 2: Create the Coating Mixture

- In a shallow dish, combine semolina, rice flour, all-purpose flour, salt, turmeric powder, and red chili powder. Mix the dry ingredients thoroughly to create the coating mixture.

Step 3: Coat the Prawns

- Heat oil in a deep frying pan or wok over medium heat. Ensure the oil is hot before adding the prawns.

- Take each marinated prawn and coat it generously with the semolina mixture. Press the coating onto the prawns to ensure it adheres well.

Step 4: Fry the Prawns

- Carefully place the coated prawns into the hot oil, ensuring not to overcrowd the pan. Fry each batch until the prawns turn golden brown and crispy. This usually takes about 2-3 minutes per batch.
- Use a slotted spoon to remove the fried prawns from the oil and place them on a plate lined with paper towels to absorb any excess oil.

Step 5: Garnish and Serve

- Garnish the Crispy Goan Prawns with fresh coriander leaves (optional) and serve hot.
- Serve with lemon wedges on the side for a burst of freshness.

Tips:

- Ensure that the oil is hot before adding the prawns to achieve a crispy coating.
- Adjust the level of spiciness by varying the amount of red chili powder in the marinade and coating mixture.
- You can experiment with the coating mixture by adding a pinch of your favorite spices like cumin or coriander for additional flavor.

Enjoy these Crispy Goan Prawns as a delightful appetizer or snack, showcasing the perfect blend of spices and the crispiness of the semolina coating that makes them irresistibly tasty.

11.Bebinca

Goan Bebinca Recipe

Ingredients

- 1 cup all-purpose flour
- 1 cup coconut milk
- 1 cup ghee (clarified butter)
- 1 1/2 cups sugar
- 6 large eggs
- 1/2 teaspoon nutmeg powder
- 1/2 teaspoon cardamom powder
- A pinch of salt

Instructions

Step 1: Prepare Ingredients

- Separate the egg yolks from the whites and keep them in separate bowls.

- In a pan, heat the ghee until it becomes liquid. Let it cool to room temperature.
- Warm the coconut milk, making sure it is not too hot. You want it to be at a temperature where you can comfortably touch it.

Step 2: Prepare the Batter

- In a large mixing bowl, combine the all-purpose flour with a pinch of salt.
- Gradually add the coconut milk to the flour, stirring continuously to avoid lumps. Make a smooth batter.
- Add the egg yolks one at a time, mixing well after each addition.
- Slowly pour in the cooled ghee while constantly stirring to incorporate it into the batter.
- Add sugar to the batter and mix until the sugar is completely dissolved.
- Lastly, add nutmeg powder and cardamom powder, giving the batter a final thorough mix.

Step 3: Beat the Egg Whites

- In a separate clean and dry bowl, beat the egg whites until stiff peaks form.
- Gently fold the beaten egg whites into the batter. This will make the Bebinca light and airy.

Step 4: Preheat the Oven

- Preheat your oven to 180°C (350°F). Grease a round baking dish with ghee or butter.

Step 5: Layering the Bebinca

- Pour a ladleful of the batter into the greased baking dish, spreading it evenly to form the first layer.
- Place the dish in the preheated oven and bake until the layer is set and turns golden brown. This usually takes about 10-12 minutes.
- Remove the dish from the oven and pour another ladleful of batter over the first layer. Again, bake until set and golden.
- Repeat this process until all the batter is used, creating multiple layers. The number of layers can vary, but traditional Bebinca has around 7-8 layers.

Step 6: Finishing Touch

- Once all the layers are done, turn on the broiler for the final layer to get a nice golden top. Keep a close eye to prevent burning, as this step is relatively quick.

Step 7: Cool and Serve

- Allow the Bebinca to cool completely before slicing. It's best served at room temperature or slightly chilled.

Tips:
- Be patient while layering. Each layer needs to set and turn golden before adding the next layer.
- You can experiment with the thickness of each layer, but keep in mind that a thinner layer cooks faster.

Bebinca is a delightful and rich Goan dessert, often enjoyed during festivals and special occasions. The layers of coconut goodness make it a unique and delicious treat that showcases the vibrant flavors of Goan cuisine. Enjoy

12.Goan Prawn Pulao

Goan Prawn Pulao Recipe

Ingredients

For Marinating the Prawns:

- 500g large prawns, cleaned and deveined
- 1 teaspoon turmeric powder
- 1 teaspoon red chili powder

- Salt to taste
- 1 tablespoon lime juice

For Pulao:

- 2 cups basmati rice, soaked for 30 minutes and drained
- 2 tablespoons oil
- 1 large onion, thinly sliced
- 2 tomatoes, chopped
- 1/2 cup coconut milk
- 1/2 cup chopped coriander leaves (cilantro) for garnish

Whole Spices:

- 2 bay leaves
- 4-5 cloves
- 4-5 green cardamom pods
- 1 cinnamon stick
- 1-star anise
- 1 teaspoon cumin seeds

Ground Spices:

- 1 teaspoon turmeric powder
- 1 teaspoon red chili powder
- 1 teaspoon coriander powder

- 1/2 teaspoon garam masala

Others:

- 4 cups water (for cooking rice)
- Salt to taste

Instructions
Step 1: Marinate the Prawns

- Clean and devein the prawns, leaving the tails intact.
- In a bowl, mix turmeric powder, red chili powder, salt, and lime juice to create a marinade.
- Coat the prawns with the marinade and let them sit for at least 15-20 minutes.

Step 2: Rinse and Soak Rice

- Rinse the basmati rice under cold water until the water runs clear.
- Soak the rice in water for about 30 minutes. Drain before use.

Step 3: Prepare Whole and Ground Spices

- In a small bowl, mix turmeric powder, red chili powder, coriander powder, and garam masala to create the ground spice mix.

- Heat oil in a heavy-bottomed pan or pot over medium heat. Add bay leaves, cloves, green cardamom pods, cinnamon stick, star anise, and cumin seeds. Sauté until the spices release their aroma.

Step 4: Sauté Onions and Tomatoes

- Add thinly sliced onions to the pot and sauté until they turn golden brown.
- Stir in chopped tomatoes and cook until they become soft and the oil starts to separate.

Step 5: Add Marinated Prawns

- Add the marinated prawns to the pot and cook until they turn pink and are almost cooked through. Remove a few prawns for garnish if desired.

Step 6: Add Ground Spice Mix

- Sprinkle the ground spice mix over the prawns and stir well to coat them with the spices.

Step 7: Add Coconut Milk

- Pour in the coconut milk, stirring to combine all the flavors.

Step 8: Cook the Rice

- Add the soaked and drained basmati rice to the pot. Stir gently to coat the rice with the flavorful mixture.
- Pour in 4 cups of water and add salt to taste. Bring the mixture to a boil.

Step 9: Simmer and Garnish

- Once it starts boiling, reduce the heat to low, cover the pot with a tight-fitting lid, and let it simmer for about 15-20 minutes or until the rice is cooked and water is absorbed.
- Once the rice is cooked, fluff it gently with a fork. Garnish with chopped coriander leaves and the reserved prawns.

Step 10: Serve

- Transfer the Goan Prawn Pulao to a serving platter. Serve hot with a side of raita or a squeeze of lime.

Tips:
- Adjust the spice levels according to your preference by varying the amount of red chili powder.
- Use fresh coconut milk for a richer flavor, or you can also use store-bought coconut milk.
- Ensure the prawns are not overcooked to maintain their tenderness and juiciness.

Enjoy this aromatic and flavorful Goan Prawn Pulao, a delightful rice dish that perfectly combines the richness of prawns with the fragrant spices of Goan cuisine. Serve it on special occasions or as a delightful main course for a family meal.

13.Pumpkin Bharta

Pumpkin Bharta Recipe

Ingredients

- 500g pumpkin, peeled and diced
- 1 cup grated coconut
- 1 tablespoon mustard seeds
- 2-3 green chilies, chopped
- 1 teaspoon turmeric powder
- 1 teaspoon red chili powder (adjust to taste)
- Salt to taste
- 2 tablespoons oil (preferably mustard oil)
- 1 teaspoon mustard seeds (for tempering)
- 1 sprig curry leaves
- Fresh coriander leaves for garnish (optional)

Instructions

Step 1: Prepare the Pumpkin

- Peel the pumpkin and remove the seeds. Cut it into small, evenly-sized cubes.

Step 2: Steam the Pumpkin

- Steam the pumpkin cubes until they are fork-tender. You can use a steamer or microwave them. Steaming helps retain the flavor and nutrients.

Step 3: Cook the Pumpkin

- In a pan, heat 2 tablespoons of oil, preferably mustard oil, over medium heat.
- Add mustard seeds to the hot oil. Allow them to splutter and release their aroma.
- Add chopped green chilies to the pan and sauté for a minute until they become fragrant.

Step 4: Add Steamed Pumpkin

- Add the steamed pumpkin cubes to the pan. Mash them with a fork or potato masher.
- Stir well to incorporate the mustard seeds and green chilies into the mashed pumpkin.

Step 5: Add Spices

- Sprinkle turmeric powder, red chili powder, and salt over the mashed pumpkin.
- Mix the spices thoroughly, ensuring they are evenly distributed.

Step 6: Add Grated Coconut

- Add grated coconut to the mashed pumpkin. The coconut adds a rich, nutty flavor to the bharta.
- Mix the coconut into the pumpkin mixture, allowing it to blend well with the spices.

Step 7: Cook the Bharta

- Cook the pumpkin bharta over low to medium heat, stirring frequently to avoid sticking. Cook until the mixture comes together and the coconut is well-incorporated. This usually takes about 10-15 minutes.

Step 8: Prepare Tempering

- In a small pan, heat a tablespoon of oil. Add mustard seeds to the hot oil.
- Once the mustard seeds splutter, add curry leaves to the tempering. Allow them to crisp up.

Step 9: Add Tempering to Bharta

- Pour the prepared tempering over the cooked pumpkin bharta. This adds an extra layer of flavor and aroma.

Step 10: Garnish and Serve

- Garnish the pumpkin bharta with fresh coriander leaves if desired.
- Serve hot as a side dish with roti, paratha, rice, or any Indian bread of your choice.

Tips:

- Adjust the spiciness by varying the quantity of green chilies and red chili powder.
- Mustard oil imparts a unique flavor to the bharta. If you find its taste too strong, you can use any other cooking oil.
- Ensure the pumpkin is well-steamed before mashing to achieve a smoother texture.

Enjoy this flavorful and nutritious Pumpkin Bharta as a side dish that brings together the natural sweetness of pumpkin, the richness of coconut, and the warmth of spices. It's a comforting dish that perfectly complements any Indian meal.

14.Goan Dal

Goan Dal Recipe

Ingredients

For Dal:

- 1 cup split pigeon peas (toor dal), washed and soaked for 30 minutes
- 1/2 cup grated coconut
- 1 small onion, finely chopped
- 1 small tomato, chopped
- 1 green chili, chopped
- 1/2 teaspoon turmeric powder
- 1 teaspoon red chili powder
- Salt to taste
- 1 tablespoon tamarind pulp
- 2 cups water

For Tempering:

- 2 tablespoons oil
- 1 teaspoon mustard seeds
- 1 teaspoon cumin seeds
- 2-3 dried red chilies
- 1 sprig curry leaves
- 1/2 teaspoon fenugreek seeds
- 1/2 teaspoon asafoetida (hing)

For Spice Paste:

- 1/2 cup grated coconut
- 1 teaspoon coriander seeds
- 1 teaspoon cumin seeds
- 4-5 black peppercorns
- 2-3 dried red chilies
- 1 small onion, chopped

Instructions
Step 1: Prepare Dal

- Wash the toor dal thoroughly and soak it in water for about 30 minutes.
- In a pressure cooker, combine the soaked dal, chopped onion, tomato, green chili, turmeric powder, red chili powder, salt, and grated coconut.
- Add 2 cups of water to the mixture. Close the pressure cooker lid and cook for 3-4 whistles or until the dal is completely cooked and soft.

Step 2: Prepare Spice Paste

- In a pan, dry roast coriander seeds, cumin seeds, black peppercorns, dried red chilies, and chopped onion until they turn golden brown. Allow them to cool.

- Once cooled, transfer the roasted spices and onion to a blender. Add grated coconut and blend into a smooth paste. Add water if needed to achieve a smooth consistency.

Step 3: Add Tamarind Pulp

- Once the dal is cooked, open the pressure cooker and mash the dal mixture using a ladle or spoon.
- Add the prepared spice paste to the dal and mix well.
- Add tamarind pulp for a tangy flavor. Adjust the quantity according to your taste preferences.

Step 4: Prepare Tempering

- In a separate pan, heat oil over medium heat for tempering.
- Add mustard seeds to the hot oil. Allow them to splutter.
- Add cumin seeds, dried red chilies, curry leaves, fenugreek seeds, and asafoetida. Sauté until the spices release their aroma.

Step 5: Add Tempering to Dal

- Pour the prepared tempering over the dal mixture. Stir well to combine all the flavors.
- Bring the dal to a gentle boil, allowing the spices to infuse into the mixture.

Step 6: Adjust Consistency

- If the dal is too thick, add some hot water to achieve the desired consistency. Stir well.

Step 7: Check Seasoning

- Taste the Goan Dal and adjust the seasoning according to your preference. Add more salt, tamarind, or red chili powder if needed.

Step 8: Simmer and Serve

- Let the dal simmer for a few more minutes, allowing all the flavors to meld together.
- Once the dal is well-cooked and has reached the desired consistency, remove it from heat.

Step 9: Garnish and Serve

- Garnish the Goan Dal with fresh coriander leaves and serve hot with steamed rice or Indian bread of your choice.

Tips:

- Adjust the spiciness by varying the quantity of dried red chilies and red chili powder.
- The tamarind pulp adds a tangy flavor, but you can adjust the quantity according to your taste preference.

- You can use other lentils like split red lentils (masoor dal) or split yellow lentils (moong dal) if toor dal is not available.

Enjoy this flavorful and comforting Goan Dal, a hearty lentil dish that brings together the richness of coconut, the tanginess of tamarind, and the aromatic Goan spices. Serve it as a main course with rice or bread for a wholesome and delicious meal.

15.Mushroom Xacuti

Mushroom Xacuti Recipe

Ingredients

For Marinating Mushrooms:

- 500g mushrooms, cleaned and quartered
- 1 teaspoon turmeric powder
- 1 teaspoon red chili powder
- Salt to taste
- 1 tablespoon lime juice

For Xacuti Masala Paste:

- 1 cup freshly grated coconut

- 1 large onion, finely chopped
- 2 medium-sized tomatoes, chopped
- 2-3 green chilies
- 1-inch ginger, chopped
- 6-8 garlic cloves
- 1 tablespoon tamarind pulp
- 1 tablespoon oil

For Roasted Spice Powder:

- 1 tablespoon coriander seeds
- 1 teaspoon cumin seeds
- 1/2 teaspoon fennel seeds
- 1/2 teaspoon poppy seeds
- 1-inch cinnamon stick
- 4-5 cloves
- 4-5 black peppercorns
- 4-5 dried red chilies (adjust according to spice preference)

For Curry:

- 2 tablespoons oil
- 1 large onion, finely sliced
- 1 teaspoon mustard seeds
- 1 sprig curry leaves

- Salt to taste
- Fresh coriander leaves for garnish

Instructions
Step 1: Marinate the Mushrooms

- Clean and quarter the mushrooms. If they are large, you can cut them into bite-sized pieces.
- In a bowl, marinate the mushrooms with turmeric powder, red chili powder, salt, and lime juice. Allow them to marinate for at least 15-20 minutes.

Step 2: Roast the Spices

- In a dry pan, roast coriander seeds, cumin seeds, fennel seeds, poppy seeds, cinnamon stick, cloves, black peppercorns, and dried red chilies over medium heat.
- Roast until the spices release their aroma and turn slightly brown. Be careful not to burn them.
- Allow the roasted spices to cool and then grind them into a fine powder using a spice grinder or mortar and pestle.

Step 3: Prepare Xacuti Masala Paste

- In the same pan, heat 1 tablespoon of oil. Add chopped onions, green chilies, ginger, and garlic. Sauté until the onions are golden brown.

- Add freshly grated coconut to the pan and roast until it turns golden brown. Stir continuously to avoid burning.
- Add chopped tomatoes and cook until they become soft and the oil starts to separate.
- Add the roasted spice powder to the pan and mix well. Cook for another 2-3 minutes.
- Allow the mixture to cool slightly. Transfer it to a blender and add tamarind pulp. Blend into a smooth paste. Add water if needed to achieve a smooth consistency.

Step 4: Cook the Mushrooms

- In a large pan or pot, heat 2 tablespoons of oil. Add mustard seeds and curry leaves. Let them splutter.
- Add sliced onions and sauté until they turn golden brown.
- Add the marinated mushrooms to the pan. Cook until the mushrooms are browned on all sides.

Step 5: Add Xacuti Masala Paste

- Pour the Xacuti masala paste into the pan with mushrooms. Mix well, ensuring that every mushroom piece is coated with the flavorful masala.

Step 6: Cook the Curry

- Add water to achieve the desired curry consistency. Bring it to a gentle boil, then reduce the heat to low and let it simmer until the mushrooms are cooked through. This usually takes about 15-20 minutes.

Step 7: Adjust Seasoning

- Taste the curry and adjust the salt according to your preference. If you like it tangier, you can add more tamarind pulp.

Step 8: Garnish and Serve

- Once the mushrooms are cooked and the curry has thickened, garnish the Mushroom Xacuti with fresh coriander leaves.
- Remove from heat and let it rest for a few minutes before serving.

Tips:
- Mushroom Xacuti is traditionally served with rice or bread. It pairs well with both white rice and Goan red rice.
- You can adjust the spice levels by varying the quantity of dried red chilies in the spice paste.

Enjoy this flavorful and aromatic Mushroom Xacuti, a vegetarian twist on the classic Goan dish, featuring the rich flavors of roasted spices, coconut, and tangy tamarind that perfectly complement the earthy taste of mushrooms. Serve it with rice or bread for a delightful meal.

May your culinary journey through the flavors of Goa be filled with joy, spice, and a dash of coastal magic! Wishing you a delightful time in the kitchen as you master the art of preparing the most popular Goan dishes. May each recipe bring the vibrant essence of Goa to your table, creating moments of culinary bliss and unforgettable feasts. Happy cooking, and may your taste buds dance to the rhythm of Goan spices

Printed in Great Britain
by Amazon

40770523R00036